C000129522

A
FATHER'S
LOVE

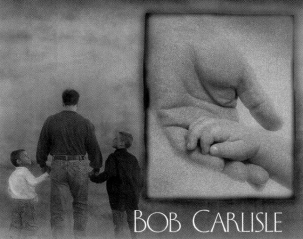

BOB CARLISLE

COUNTRYMAN

Introduction

Over the past year, the one question I've been asked more than any other is, "When are you going to write a song for your son?" After thinking of several titles like "Get Down Offa That" or "Butterfly Stitches," I came up with "A Father's Love."

I hesitated to release a song for my son because I did not want to be perceived as trying to milk the success of his sister's song. But the truth is, I wouldn't cut a slice of cake for one child and not cut an equal slice for the other. So I recorded "A Father's Love" for Evan Carlisle. The song talks about the fact that there is no greater love than the love that both Jesus and I have for him.

I love my children for completely equal, yet for completely different reasons. I am not trying to be a father to the world, I am just trying to be a father to Brooke and Evan . . . and let the world look in from time to time.

My prayer is that men will read the thoughts in this book that other men have shared about their sons and possibly be able to relate to the various situations written on these pages. By doing so, maybe each will be able to share their own "Father's Love" memories with that special son in their life before time gets away from them. If this happens, then the book and the song will have done all I hoped they would. Sometimes to grow, we need to be a little transparent.

BOB CARLISLE
OCTOBER 1998

A Father's Love

BY BOB CARLISLE AND RANDY THOMAS

Three feet tall, and full of questions
You must have thought I was the smartest man alive
I didn't always have the answers
To every little how and where and why
Like *Daddy, why's the sky so blue today?*
Does Jesus really hear me when I pray?
When I grow up, will I be just like you?
Will I be tall and strong and brave?

CHORUS:

There is no power on earth like your father's love
So big and so strong as your father's love
A promise that's sacred, a promise from heaven above
No matter where you go . . . always know
You can depend on your father's love.

Especially when it's cold, especially when you're lonely
When your little heart is just trying to find it's way
I know the world is always changing
But just remember, son, that some things never change
So even when my time on earth is through
There still will be a part of me in you
'Cause some things are forever
Nothing's ever gonna take my love from you

SECOND CHORUS:

There is no power on earth like your father's love
So big and so strong as your father's love
A promise that's sacred, a promise from heaven above
Did I hug enough? Did I care enough?
When you most needed me,
Was I there enough?
Enough to make you feel the power of your father's love?

I Was Wrong

Joseph won eight basketball college scholarships, but he chose to attend Vanderbuilt University without a scholarship because that was where he *wanted* to go.

He chose to sell books door-to-door in a summer program. He was shy, and I thought he would not last the first week. How wrong I was! Not only was he successful, but he was number one in sales! Then I knew he was an ace, and I knew he was good.

After graduate school, he said our company needed to diversify or we would not grow. I thought to myself, *he just got his MBA and he thinks he know all about business.* However, with Joe in the lead, our gift division has become more profitable than I could have imagined. So, I was wrong again!

My son and I have had a special relationship these thirty-six years. Like General McArthur, my prayer has been, "Lord, build me a son . . . who will be proud and unbending in honest defeat and humble and gentle in victory."

God has answered my prayers.

SAM MOORE

A Message of Love

My father has always shown me unconditional love. This is a love that has strengthened every aspect of my life.

From little league pep talks to words of encouragement as a new father, he has always believed in me. Belief and confidence are heart-felt emotions that he has freely shared.

During my summers in college, like my father, I sold books door-to-door. By the second week, feeling lonely and rejected, I tried to rationalize why I had taken that job. I called my dad and asked how he had handled the rejection. He said, "Son, believe in selling's law of averages. Tomorrow will be a new day. Control what you can—your attitude. I know you will have a great day and a great summer."

Most of that conversation has faded from my memory, but the message is still vivid—not so much what he was saying as what his heart was saying: "I love you and I believe in you."

Now, with children of my own, I realize more than ever the importance of that message.

JOSEPH MOORE

A Great and Wonderful Thing!

My boy is twelve years old, that place between childhood and adolescence where there are only a few important things: playing with the guys, his dog, and his dad. I am pleased to be on his short list. We made a deal years ago when he was six that he would not be embarrassed to kiss me, even when he turned eighteen. So far, he has held to the bargain.

Lately, Carl has taken up golf. I would have preferred that he stay with baseball, where my job was coaching loudly from the parent's bench, but he discovered the joy of the golf swing. I feel his satisfaction in having me with him when he turns to me after a good hit as if to say, "See that, Dad?" I am overwhelmed that my opinion means so much to him.

It is my good fortune, as I watch him grow, to be a participant in the glow of his affection. It's a great and wonderful thing!

RAY WARE

Dad Likes Everything About Me

My dad is a normal guy who knows how to have fun. He loves to have "adventures." When I was five, we jumped on our bikes and told everyone we were going on an adventure. I had to peddle fast to keep up since I had no idea where this adventure would lead us.

One time we ended up in an orange grove. We picked fresh oranges, looked at each other enjoying the juice, and made up stories about where we were and how we got there.

On our latest adventure, we tipped our kayak over twice in the Gulf of Mexico and lost all the rented scuba gear. I was scared until Dad made it into an adventure. Then I forgot to be afraid.

The thing about my dad is that he doesn't criticize me or make me do things a certain way. He likes everything about me. He's the best Dad in the whole world.

CARL WARE

Learning About God's Heart

I love watching Evan when he doesn't know I'm looking. Maybe he's just watching television or playing his guitar or doing his homework. I study his face and marvel at how he has his mom's hair, my nose, her eyes, my chin, her mouth. I'm in awe of the fact that God has allowed Jacque and I to have even a small taste of what it feels like to have created someone in our own image. It only serves to remind me how overwhelmingly loved we are by our Heavenly Father.

Two of the greatest honors of my life were to baptize my daughter and to stand at the altar with my son as he asked Jesus to come into his heart. Jacque and I haven't always known how to be good parents, but we knew enough to lead our children to the Cross. There is no greater satisfaction.

It overwhelms me when Evan says, "I want to be like you, Dad." I think of all the things that I know to be right and of all the things I know I've done wrong. Evan makes me want to do better. Words can hardly begin to express the love I have for my son.

Just last night as we prayed together, Evan prayed, not for himself, but for the new kids at school—those who haven't made many friends yet. What a heart! How fortunate these kids will be to have Evan Carlisle as their friend!

Hopefully, through his mother and me, Evan will learn more of God's love. Through Evan, I am learning more about God's heart.

BOB CARLISLE

My Dad, My Best Friend

My dad and I are best friends as well as father and son. In the song, "A Father's Love," he shares his passion for me, so I would like to share my love for him.

Dad, you taught me how to brush my teeth, how to talk, how to use the restroom, and much more. You protect me from things and people that would hurt me.

Thanks for writing this song for me. You wanted to show your love for me, and it worked! The part that really gets to me is *"when my life on earth is through, there will always be a part of me in you."*

I love you with all my heart, mind, and soul, and never want to be without you. I hope I grow up to be like you. I think I'm like you now because we share a love of music. Some day, Daddy, I want to write a song to you!

EVAN CARLISLE
(eleven years old)

Tough Love

When our son Chad was in his late teens, his defiant attitude and rebellious spirit tested me to the limits. Since his birth I have wanted to have a close relationship with him. I did not realize that a relationship like that had to begin with me.

When he would frustrate me, I would get on him and would make him angry. This created a barrier between us. When my rotten attitude changed, my son's attitude changed. I learned a valuable lesson when I discovered how to give my son "the blessing."

He is now twenty-nine and is serving a sixteen-year prison sentence (he was found guilty by association—he was in the wrong place at the wrong time), but God has given me a special love for my son that is beyond description.

BILL CHAFFIN

From Prison . . .

When I was twelve years old, my Dad made a wrong decision that sent him to prison for 849 days. The hardship he brought to our family made me very angry. I needed the companionship of my father.

I became a loner. I went to Alaska and joined the Air Force at age eighteen. A marriage that lasted only seven months fell apart. I went from one job to another. The dreams I once had were shattered.

When I was twenty-five, I started serving a prison sentence. Who was there for me? My father! He has been with me through this struggle and has expressed forgiveness and real love for me. Healing has taken place in our relationship.

Although I am locked up physically, I feel free mentally, emotionally, and spiritually. And . . . **my dad is now my hero!**

CHAD CHAFFIN

God's Gift

Jonathan means "God has given," and He truly did give our son as a gift to Anne and me. Today he is a physical giant of a man at six feet nine inches tall, but he is also a spiritual giant. His physical growth can be attributed to his enormous appetite, but his spiritual growth, in part, comes from the prayers of his grandparents, his mother and myself, and our friends. Jonathan's spiritual appetite has always been large. As a child he would listen intently to the Bible stories I would read each night, and then he would relay them to his sisters and friends with zeal and confident faith.

Jonathan has never hidden his light under a bushel. From grade school through college, he has been a warrior for the Lord. My son's love for me has overwhelmed me with the love of the Son of God. He is my best friend. I am assured that He who began a good work in him will continue to mold and make him into a giant for God in his generation.

DANNY LOTZ

Dad's Powerful Example

No one has had more influence on me than my dad. He taught me how to shoot a free throw, throw a football, study for an algebra exam, teach a Sunday school class, stand up for what is right even when no one else does . . . and the list goes on.

But the main thing Dad taught me is that there is nothing in this world that means more to him than his relationship with Jesus. One of the first Bible verses I memorized as a little boy was Matthew 6:33, "Seek first the kingdom of God and His righteousness, and all these things shall be added to you."

Although my dad taught me a lot, there is nothing more prevalent in my mind than the powerful testimony that he has lived out so faithfully before me during my twenty-eight years. My dad's greatest influence has been his faithfulness in teaching me about Jesus Christ—the *real* influence.

JONATHAN LOTZ

THREE FEET TALL, AND FULL OF QUESTIONS

*You must have thought
I was the smartest man alive*

I DIDN'T ALWAYS HAVE THE ANSWERS
TO EVERY LITTLE HOW AND WHERE AND WHY

*Like Daddy,
why's the sky so blue today?*

DOES JESUS REALLY HEAR ME WHEN I PRAY?

WHEN I GROW UP, WILL I BE JUST LIKE YOU?

*Will I be tall
and strong and brave?*

THERE IS NO POWER ON EARTH LIKE YOUR FATHER'S LOVE

So big and so strong
as your father's love

A PROMISE THAT'S SACRED,
A PROMISE FROM HEAVEN ABOVE

No matter where you go . . .
always know

YOU CAN DEPEND ON YOUR FATHER'S LOVE

To My Four Sons,

I've never met another father with two sets of twin sons. Being your father has been, for this and other reasons, a remarkable experience. As my youngest children have now passed their twenty-first birthday, my role and perspectives are changing. Allow me to share some thoughts with you at this point in my journey.

One of the many blessings of such a large family, with "multiple sets of multiples," is the evidence such an experience provides of our individuality. Your mother and I have learned well that each of you are both unique and yet equal in God's eyes, as you are in ours. Though we provided almost identical genetics and environment, you each developed your own personality and gifts. I can see something of myself in each of you, and yet, collectively, you have so much more to offer. Your attributes and achievements wonderfully compliment each other.

I respect each of you for who you are and am thankful for your differences. Just as you struggled to separate yourselves as young siblings, when you were always considered a "matched pair," I pray that you will now strive to grow closer as adults. Each of you can uniquely honor God. So appreciate and *love* each other as only brothers can.

That simple four letter word deserves comment. Framed on my bathroom wall, positioned so that I must see it each morning as I shave, is a principle I have learned to live by, "Love is a decision." Our world defines love in many ways but rarely, if ever, as a decision. Yet God commands us to love Him and one another. We make conscious choices every day whether to obey that commandment. There will be days when you don't feel loving toward your job, your wife, your family, or your God. Yet, we are not requested to love, we are commanded to love.

Consistent loving behavior reflects integrity, builds character, and channels feelings. At those times when feelings fail you—and they will—be led by your decision to love.

I am proud of each of you. I am blessed by each of you. I will continue to be your father—I look forward to becoming your friend.

YOUR DAD,
JOHN LOGSDON

Dear Dad,

I want you to know how much I have taken you for granted. As a child, I expected you to read with me at night, to watch cartoons with me, and stay up all night with me when I was sick.

In my teenage years, I expected you to provide me with a car, to wait up for me on weekends, and to be the only father to attend football practice during the week—even though that meant getting home later at night.

All of these expectations were second nature to me and did not require conscious thought, but now I think you planned it that way.

As a young man with a new wife and career, I have begun to appreciate the amount of energy and love it must have taken for you to create those expectations in five children. With each passing day, I appreciate you more and more. When I am a father, I only hope that I am able to create half of the expectations that you created in me.

Your Son,
Mark Logsdon

Dear Dad,

Traveling around the city today in search of a suitable location for our wedding seemed to flood my memory with images of my past. I suppose that facing the reality of such a momentous occasion should prompt a re-evaluation of one's life up to that point. So many thoughts and emotions came to mind. But through it all, it struck me how intricately your presence was woven into that fabric.

I see you standing on the sidelines when I score a goal on the soccer field, or when I'm running the quarterback and getting sacked. You're in the audience when I receive my M.D. and when I play out of sequence with the orchestra. There were so many anxious phone calls and questions that you had to endure when I left home and struggled with loneliness and my place in the world. But through the haze of uncertainty I could always see the pattern you had left me. Of course it wasn't always perfect, but it was honorable and unique. My hope and prayer is that you can see such a pattern in my life.

There's a Roman saying that reminds me of you, "The way of a father is to accustom his son to do the right thing of his own accord." Thanks, Dad, for your loving presence in my life.

LOVE,
MATTHEW LOGSDON

Dear Dad,

About a month ago, as Jeremy and I were sitting on a train on our way back from a day-trip in England, we realized that we could possible be two of the luckiest guys on earth. There we were, in England for a month, to "study abroad," and to have the experience of a lifetime. You know, twenty-one-year-old college kids really cannot ask for much more than that for their birthday. But, the fact that we were in London, staying at Westminister Abbey, honestly was not the reason for our overwhelming sense of thanksgiving. Having a father that was willing to provide so much in order that his youngest twin boys could have such an experience, was the reason for our gratitude. So Jeremy and I felt like writing you a letter to express our complete appreciation for your love and commitment to us. Of course, there is no way that we can give thanks for all the wonderful things you have done for us, but we felt that we would try anyway.

As we watched the landscape zoom by, so many memories of our youth resurfaced in our minds. Memories of times in our childhood when we felt scared or alone, and just before we began to wonder if all hope had been lost you would be there with a smile on your face and a sparkle in your eye. Time and time again you sacrificed work to make it to our football and basketball games, even though you really didn't have enough time. You were always there to cheer us on, even if we did something wrong. You were always there to pick us up when we fell. Father, you have so many amazing qualities that make you the man we so dearly adore. Your unconditional love and support, the habit of always putting others in front of yourself, and your positive attitude are just a few of your marvelous qualities.

Jeremy and I have been able to accomplish so many feats and have had the opportunity to have such incredible experiences in our lives. Without the lessons that you taught us through loving support and faith, our lives would have been a lot different. Isaac Newton once  said, "The reason I can see so far is because I stand on the shoulders of giants." Father, you are a giant in our lives. So many people have told us that because there are two sets of twins in our family that makes us special, or difficult, or unique. I used to get so tired of hearing that. Sometimes I would get angry and say, "Our family is just like everyone else's family!" But, as I was sitting on that train, thousands of miles from home, I realized that all along those people were right; we are different. Our family is special, not because of our two sets of twins but because of our extraordinary father and mother. So thank you Father for raising us in the loving manner that you did. However, more importantly, Jeremy and I give thanks to God for blessing us with a remarkable man to be an example to help guide the way.

LOVE FROM YOUR SONS,
JOSEPH AND JEREMY LOGSDON

I Remember My Son . . .

In his early childhood, the privilege I had of leading him to salvation in Jesus Christ and the growth of that relationship as his faith has matured.

When he faced a difficult decision as a young adult and sought the Lord's guidance. The Lord was glorified as a result of his choice.

The day he decided he wanted to follow in my footsteps and become a salesman.

When he chose to join our family business, one of my lifetime dreams came true. Now we can pray together for decisions to be made about the business, and I have a wonderful opportunity to disciple and train him.

The day he played miniature golf when he was three or four years old and made a hole in one, two different times.

The day his Anne Marie was born—he walked into the hospital nursery with her in his arms and tears in his eyes.

I love him and am proud that he is my son. I thank God for allowing me to be his father.

WOODY WOJDYLAK

My Good-Luck Charm

My dad is a great worker, boss, and friend. He taught me as a young boy to work hard at whatever you put your mind to and you will be successful.

He taught me about the outdoors, camping, fishing, and hunting, where we have had some great bonding times. He and Mom taught me about right and wrong, God and Jesus. I am grateful for their guidance.

Not long ago, during deer season, he was trimming trees around his cabin. He fell off the ladder and had to go to the emergency room for a few stitches. A little while later I got my first deer. I plan to call him to trim trees again next year at deer season. I called him my good-luck charm.

Now that I am a father, I hope I will be a great dad as well. I love my dad, and I am thankful to God for him.

MARK WOJDYLAK

I'm Praying for You

Curtis, I pray for such a joy for you as you consider your choices for law school. I pray that the Holy Spirit will reveal to you the most essential element in your decision making process: intimacy with our Heavenly Father like you have never known before.

He will give you choices in order to grow your faith. He can and will use you no matter where you decide to attend. The decision that you and He make will give you peace and assurance that the light you are following is what He has provided and not some light that you have made to shine. Don't follow your own natural, human emotions or understanding—and spend time in prayer before you decide.

Your work should be viewed as your ministry. Oswald Chambers once said, "Joy comes from the complete fulfillment of the specific purpose for which you are created and born again."

I LOVE YOU. I'M PROUD OF YOU. I'M PRAYING FOR YOU.

SEALY YATES

I Appreciate Your Efforts

You have been a wonderful father to me. You have taught by example, sacrificed for me, supported me, imparted wisdom to me, consoled me, prayed with me—especially when my roommate, Patrick, broke his neck when I flipped him over my back. The words you shared with me from your journal and from your insight have been encouraging, comforting, and uplifting. I have read and reread your words to me after this accident and cannot tell you how much they have meant to me at this trying time.

I have also learned about hard work, integrity, love, discipline, and about following Jesus just by watching you. I appreciate your efforts and your openness with me.

As I move closer to marriage, parenting, and a career, I want to spend more time discussing what you have learned from your experiences.

THANKS FOR ALL YOU HAVE DONE FOR ME.
I LOVE YOU DAD.
CURTIS YATES

My Son—My Delight

Our two daughters were ten and five when Joel was born. When he was a baby, they treated him like he was their own child. He was five years old before he realized that he didn't have three mothers! His sisters instilled in him a sense of loving and caring that has never compromised his masculinity.

Joel has excelled in baseball, basketball, soccer, and golf. I have had the fortune to either coach him or assist in most of the sports he has been involved in. At thirteen his hands are as big as his dad's, his feet are bigger than his dad's, and he is taller than all three "moms."

He has matured into a godly young man who is not afraid to ask theological questions in Sunday school or to pray in public. It is a comfort and a delight to have a teenage son who is not embarrassed to give his mom or dad a kiss or hug in public—not even in front of his friends.

DAVID DUNHAM

My Dad Will Listen

My dad is a busy man. He is forever on the phone or the computer. He has a cell phone and a pager. He says, "Busy is good because *not* busy means no work." Sometimes he will take one of us kids on a business trip with him. Our reward for sitting still and being polite to grown-ups is being able to be alone with him.

Family vacations are usually in convention cities. After meetings, Dad joins us for a week of sightseeing and play. Once in Seattle, we swam and fished one day and threw snowballs the next—in August! We used tents, campfires, and didn't bathe for a week!

Some Saturdays, Dad will wake one of us up to go have breakfast, one on one. He catches up on our week and tells stories about when he was young.

The best thing about my dad is that he will listen, and nothing is too dumb or too stupid to talk to him about.

JOEL DUNHAM

They're Grown Up

My number-one son, Timothy Brian, has been like me—stubborn. He is built like me too, only stronger. We clashed a lot when he was growing up, but now we have a very good relationship. We almost lost him in a terrible car accident just after high school. Looking at Tim in the hospital with all those tubes in him caused us so much pain. It was almost unbearable. But with God's strength we all got through it. Today, he and I play golf together and enjoy each other very much.

Growing up, Christopher Edward, my number-two son was sweet and caring. He cared about how others felt in a unique way. If he could make someone feel better, he would. In high school he worked for a small hospital for the mentally disabled. He would take small groups of them to the theater and other places. Those actions made me very proud of him. Today, Chris is still a caring person and goes the extra mile to bring a smile to someone who needs it.

ED PLUMMER

It Pays to Listen to Dad

Dad has "been there and done that." He's shown me a lot. I appreciate him more as I get older. He has encouraged me to get involved in many things. We love to be together and do stuff. He likes to party. Who can keep up with him? He's a fun guy! His elk sausage spaghetti is delicious!

Dad is also my confidant, and it pays me to listen well to him. I love my dad.

TIM PLUMMER

Dad and I would go fishing most Saturdays. One time the ocean was alive with fish and very rough. The wind was blowing, and the boat was rolling. Dad sensed something was wrong and started to head back to shore. Then the drive shaft broke, and we were left without a motor. I was scared, but Dad assured me that everything would be okay. He called the coast guard for help, all the time still fishing. They came to our rescue and towed us back to the harbor—while we were still fishing! Dad turned a scary event into one of the happiest memories of my life.

CHRIS PLUMMER

My Boys

When I think of my boys, Bret and Jason, my heart is full, for they are young men of character and strength. Each is different in his own way, but they are the same when it comes to accepting a challenge or accomplishing a responsibility.

I can remember how Bret as a young boy was always curious about things and his mother would answer every question. Jason had an adventurous, free spirit and would never finish a meal at a restaurant with the family because he would wander off to discover people and places he had never seen before.

Today, life and opportunity is before each of them and, God willing, they will find that the only true happiness in life is a moment–by–moment relationship with Jesus Christ.

I love them both unconditionally and pray that we will have many more great times together, whether on the golf course or hanging out with my sons and grandson.

JACK COUNTRYMAN

Dad's Winning Team

My father is a leader on the playing field, at church, on the job, and in life. He leads from the top by example.

He has been there for me at meetings, at games, in conversations. He has lifted me up. He is a pillar of strength for me.

When I was eighteen, he told me that I didn't know it all. That was a surprise as well as a powerful lesson. One reason for success in my life has been when I have listened. He said, "No one ever listened himself out of a sale, but you can talk yourself out of one!"

Winning breeds success. Dad, I love you very much, and I am proud to be on your winning team in life.

BRET COUNTRYMAN

To me, Dad, you are the greatest! You are a great father, provider, and best friend. You are courageous and loving. Though you traveled a lot, you were always there for me twenty-four hours a day, seven days a week by phone or in person.

I have a family of my own now, but I still look to you for guidance. As I continue to grow, I want to be like your example of a father, provider, and best friend. I love you Dad; you are "the man."

JASON COUNTRYMAN

ESPECIALLY WHEN IT'S COLD,

ESPECIALLY WHEN YOU'RE LONELY

When your little heart

is just trying to find it's way

I KNOW THE WORLD IS ALWAYS CHANGING

BUT JUST REMEMBER, SON, THAT SOME THINGS NEVER CHANGE

So even when my time on earth is through

There still will be a part of me in you

'CAUSE SOME THINGS ARE FOREVER

NOTHING'S EVER GONNA TAKE MY LOVE FROM YOU

THERE IS NO POWER ON EARTH LIKE YOUR FATHER'S LOVE

SO BIG AND SO STRONG AS YOUR FATHER'S LOVE

A promise that's sacred,

a promise from heaven above

DID I HUG ENOUGH?

DID I CARE ENOUGH?

When you most needed Me

Was I there enough?

ENOUGH TO MAKE YOU FEEL

THE POWER OF YOUR FATHER'S LOVE?

My Five Sons

Challenges occurred when God and my wife presented me with five sons (though not all at once). I am just an average guy. I don't have a photographic memory, am not athletically gifted, don't have wisdom beyond my years. How could I hold my sons to these standards? I merely learned to build a road map for them based on integrity, industry, persistence, and perseverance.

My sons were born with strengths and weaknesses. I have encouraged their capabilities and strengths and taught them how to overcome or live with their weaknesses. I accept them unconditionally and they accept me unconditionally.

We have grown together through paper routes at four a.m., schools, sports, hunting, and fishing. Always together, always a team.

They have responded to my life's plan for them by growing into men who are my friends, companions, support teams, counselors, and sounding boards.

They have strong opinions, are perceptive, and have become accomplished Christian individuals. They are wise and well thought of in their chosen professions.

They never cease to amaze me. I awake every day with a prayer of thanksgiving for my five sons.

Bob Naughton

Dad,

You are energetic, entertaining, adventurous, rugged, responsible, fun to be with, and have a positive attitude. You never give up. You strive to do your best in everything. You taught us to have respect for others. You are faithful to Mom, and you are our number one role model!

MIKE NAUGHTON

My father who art in Houston, honored be thy name, thy new house come, Mom's will be done on earth as it is in Heaven. Give us this wedding trip, our daily bread, forgive us our indebtedness—cause we'll never be able to pay you back. And lead us down the aisle at Big Bear and deliver us from the bill. For thine is the truest heart and the power of gratitude.

JOE NAUGHTON

You used patience when you taught all five of us to play soccer and to play golf. There were times when you could have gone out with "the guys" but you taught us by your example to do what is best for your family, not what is easiest for yourself!

You went to great lengths to ensure that all five of us lived in an environment that provided challenges for us to overcome. You helped build confidence in us so we would be able to face our future in a more mature world.

SCOTT NAUGHTON

You have dedicated your whole life to your family, and you expected nothing in return. You committed your life to God and to us and to Mom. Your love for us is like God's love for us . . . unconditional. Our family is very blessed.

I have seen the Scriptures lived out where fathers are told to be good examples of Christian living so that the young men can see how it is done. My future wife will not be able to thank you enough for the way you raised me and the example you set.

KEN NAUGHTON

I have loved you all my life. I had the best childhood because of you and Mom. In recent years, when we started hunting together, just you and me, I felt that we had become great friends.

You hugged me the first time this year at church, and it felt very good. I have not said this to you in the twenty-two years I have lived, so . . . "I love you!" I owe you everything. You gave me everything. Don't ever die, I want to keep you in my life as long as I can.

DAN NAUGHTON

Stubborn as Mules

Our jeep was coming down the Montana road with no driver! As I ran after it, it left the pavement and stopped in a field. Out popped our six-year-old son, Frankie, and his three-year-old sister. He ran away, and I couldn't catch him. I took his sister home and locked all the doors. As Frankie tried to get in the door, I jumped out to catch

him but he was too fast. Later his sister was talking to him out the window. One jump from me and I finally caught him. I didn't punish him because I was so relieved he was not hurt.

I figured our eight-year-old son, Jerry Jr., (who watched them drive off) taught Frankie how to put that jeep in reverse. My sons were smart, stubborn as mules, and had minds of their own. They were raised to be loyal, independent, and passionate about their dreams.

Now they are grown and the house is too quiet, too clean, and too big without them. I am proud of them and love them dearly. They have exceeded my expectations.

JERRY PAPE

I Hope I Am Just Like Him

My dad listens to everything I say, even though he pretends not to. He tells me "no" when he means "yes." He acts like he is not concerned, but he always asks my mother how I am doing. He loves to compete with me, but I know he is happier when I win. He pretends he is too busy to do something with me, but then he will make time for me. I think I should tell him that he is my best friend. I hope I am just like him someday.

FRANK PAPE

Dad, you have never been affected by what people think of you, and you taught me not to be limited by what people think of me. You've always been supportive of me in spite of the mistakes I've made.

You adore children and animals, and that is when your emotional non-rugged side shows. I know you love me even though you yell and scream sometimes and are slightly temperamental. What I've needed, you've always provided. You've made me believe I can do anything I want to do.

JERRY PAPE JR.

From a Stepfather

The woman I had fallen in love with had a young son, Chris. For our situation, we both agreed that it was very important that Chris also want me in his life. If not, Kathryn and I would not get married. I found that he was a great kid who was easy to love and who gave love in return.

The love I feel for him surprises me, and on some days I have to remind myself that I am not his biological father. He and I have come to understand that I will never replace his father, but a gracious God has given us the ability to love one another in a special way that springs from our choice to accept each other and to build on our relationship daily before Him. I am very grateful.

GEORGE KING

From a Stepson

It was real sad when my parents got divorced. I was eight years old and was freaked out for a while. We moved to a new town, and I left all my friends. I wasn't happy. It was rough, but we survived.

Mom dated but never brought anybody home. She said she would never marry anyone I did not get along with. I wasn't thrilled about her dating but definitely did *not* want her to remarry!

Then she started dating George. He seemed cool, liked kids, and has two grown kids of his own. We like the same things, and he always includes me. We talk about things only guys talk about. I love and respect him, and we have a great relationship.

He and my mom got married two years ago. We are all very happy.

CHRIS JACOBS
(fourteen years old)

My World Fell Apart

"Dad, will you help me put my bike together?" These words led to one blinding moment when my whole world fell apart. My son and I brought the carton into the kitchen and began to undo the packing. David got a knife from the drawer and jabbed and pulled at the box. With lightning speed, the sharp point of the knife went into the center of his cornea and split open his eye.

As I rushed him to the hospital my world was in despair, and I did not think I could ever be happy again. I cried out to God. With this injury to my son, the only place I could look was up.

The Lord has provided for all our needs. David did not lose his eye nor his eyesight. With the help of a mar-velous physician and a contact lens, he can see past the scar that formed on his eye surface.

The years I have had of memorizing Scriptures brings me peace and assures me that one day, in Eternity, David's eye will be whole.

HANK HANEGRAAFF

Dear Dad,

I love you very much, and I look forward to going to France with you. You are the best dad ever, and I am very proud of you. You have accomplished so much, and you have impacted so many people's lives, and on top of that you are the best golfer I know! I love you very much, and I am very proud to have you as my Dad.

If I have questions about the Bible, you can give me a long answer. You help me memorize the verses. I really like having the "'Bible Answer Man" as my father! From the time of my eye accident when I was three, to this day, when I need you, you are always there.

YOUR SON,
DAVID HANEGRAAFF